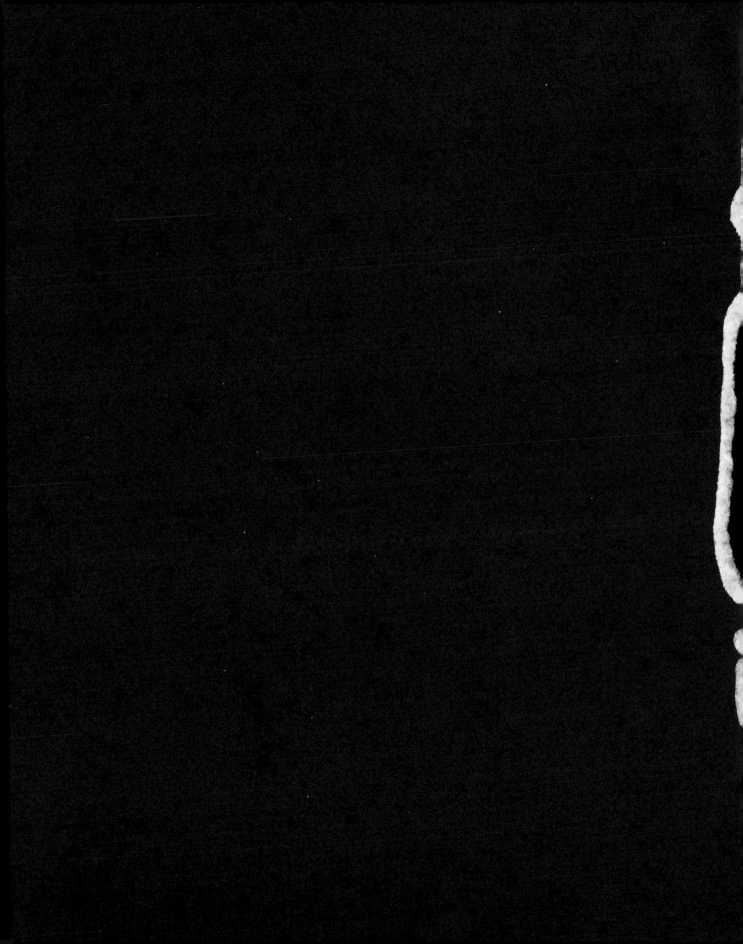

SONGS FROM GREEN PASTURES

Selections from the Psalms
in The New King James Version

Text by
Jill and Stuart Briscoe

Thomas Nelson Publishers
Nashville

Photographs copyright © 1981 by Forlaget Scandinavia, Copenhagen, Denmark

Text copyright © 1982 by Thomas Nelson, Inc., Publishers

The Scripture quotations in this publication are from The New King
James Version. Copyright © 1979, 1980, 1982, Thomas Nelson, Inc., Publishers.

Published in Nashville, Tennessee, by Thomas
Nelson, Inc., Publishers and distributed in Canada
by Lawson Falle, Ltd., Cambridge, Ontario.

Text selections followed by the initials JB are by Jill Briscoe.
Text selections followed by the initials SB are by Stuart Briscoe.

ISBN 0-8407-4101-4

SONGS FROM
GREEN PASTURES

Selections from the Psalms

The Law of the LORD

The heavens declare the glory of God;
And the firmament shows His handiwork.
Day unto day utters speech,
And night unto night reveals knowledge.
There is no speech nor language
Where their voice is not heard.
Their line has gone out through all the earth,
And their words to the end of the world. . . .
The law of the LORD is perfect,
converting the soul;
The testimony of the LORD is sure,
making wise the simple;
The statutes of the LORD are right,
rejoicing the heart;
The commandment of the LORD is
pure, enlightening the eyes;
The fear of the LORD is clean,
enduring forever;
The judgments of the LORD are true
and righteous altogether.
More to be desired are they than gold,
Yea, than much fine gold;
Sweeter also than honey and the honeycomb.
Moreover by them Your servant is warned,
And in keeping them there is great reward.
Who can understand his errors?
Cleanse me from secret faults.
Keep back Your servant also from
presumptuous sins;
Let them not have dominion over me.
Then I shall be blameless,
And I shall be innocent of great transgression.
Let the words of my mouth and the
meditation of my heart
Be acceptable in Your sight,
O LORD, my strength and my redeemer.
[verses 1–4, 7–14]

The world is so full of noise, so many voices clamoring for my attention. In the midst of the confusion, I love the cool, calm sanity of Your truth. Your laws speak strong wisdom to my heart; they bring sweet delight to my life. —SB

Trust and Remember

May the LORD answer you in the day of trouble;
May the name of the God of Jacob defend you;
May He send you help from the sanctuary,
And strengthen you out of Zion;
May He remember all your offerings,
And accept your burnt sacrifice.   Selah
May He grant you according to your heart's desire,
And fulfill all your purpose.
We will rejoice in your salvation,
And in the name of our God we will
set up our banners!
May the LORD fulfill all your petitions.
Now I know that the LORD saves His anointed;
He will answer him from His holy heaven
With the saving strength of His right hand.
Some trust in chariots, and some in horses;
But we will remember the name of the LORD our God.
They have bowed down and fallen;
But we have risen and stand upright.
Save, LORD!
May the King answer us when we call.

*It is hard for us to trust in a God
we cannot see. As we hear of wars and rumors
of wars, we are tempted to put our faith in the
modern war machine, forgetting that "the king's
heart is in the hand of the Lord, and He turns
it withersoever He will." Father, help us
to remember Your chosen Christ
is KING OF KINGS
and LORD OF LORDS!* —JB

The Blessings of Goodness

The king shall have joy in Your strength, O LORD;
And in Your salvation how greatly shall he rejoice!
You have given him his heart's desire,
And have not withheld the request of his lips.   Selah
For You meet him with the blessings of goodness;
You set a crown of pure gold upon his head.
He asked life from You,
And You gave it to him—
Length of days forever and ever.
His glory is great in Your salvation;
Honor and majesty You have placed upon him.
For You have made him most blessed forever;
You have made him exceedingly glad
With Your presence.
For the king trusts in the LORD,
And through the mercy of the Most High
He shall not be moved.
Your hand will find all Your enemies;
Your right hand will find those who hate You.
You shall make them as a fiery oven in the time
Of Your anger;
The LORD shall swallow them up in His wrath,
And the fire shall devour them.
Their offspring You shall destroy from the earth,
And their descendants from among the sons of men.
For they intended evil against You;
They devised a plot which they are not
Able to perform.
Therefore You will make them turn their back;
You will make ready Your arrows on
Your string toward their faces.
Be exalted, O LORD, in Your own strength!
We will sing and praise Your power.

*Immaturity thinks it can ask God to give it
the desires of its heart, expecting to receive
everything it wants! Maturity knows better,
choosing rather to have its heart filled with
the very desires of God Himself.
Lord, make us mature. —JB*

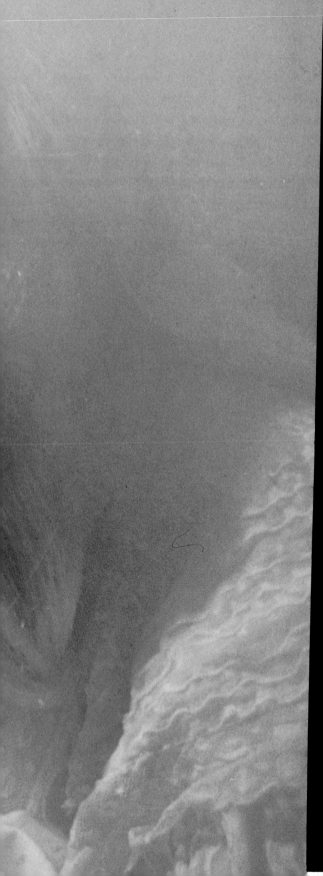

The Silence of God

My God, My God, why have You forsaken Me?
Why are You so far from helping Me,
And from the words of My groaning?
O My God, I cry in the daytime,
but You do not hear;
And in the night season, and am not silent.
But You are holy,
Who inhabit the praises of Israel.
Our fathers trusted in You;
They trusted, and You delivered them.
They cried to You, and were delivered;
They trusted in You, and were not ashamed.
But I am a worm, and no man;
A reproach of men, and despised of the people.
All those who see Me laugh Me to scorn;
They shoot out the lip, they shake the head, saying,
"He trusted in the LORD, let Him rescue Him;
Let Him deliver Him, since He delights in Him!"
But You are He who took Me out of the womb;
You made Me trust when I was on My
mother's breasts.
I was cast upon You from birth.
From My mother's womb
You have been My God.
Be not far from Me,
For trouble is near;
For there is none to help. [verses 1–11]

The difficulties of life sometimes threaten
to tear me apart. But I remember the wonder
of my conception, the miracle of my birth,
the security of Your care in the days of
my infant weakness. These thoughts remind me
to count on Your presence. —SB

From PSALM 22

You Have Answered Me

For dogs have surrounded Me;
The assembly of the wicked has enclosed Me.
They pierced My hands and My feet;
I can count all My bones.
They look and stare at Me.
They divide My garments among them,
And for My clothing they cast lots.
But You, O LORD, do not be far from Me;
O My Strength, hasten to help Me!
Deliver Me from the sword,
My precious life from the power of the dog.
Save Me from the lion's mouth
And from the horns of the wild oxen!
You have answered Me.
I will declare Your name to My brethren;
In the midst of the congregation I will praise You.
You who fear the LORD, praise Him!
All you descendants of Jacob, glorify Him,
And fear Him, all you offspring of Israel!
For He has not despised nor abhorred
the affliction of the afflicted;
Nor has He hidden His face from Him;
But when He cried to Him, He heard. . . .
The poor shall eat and be satisfied;
Those who seek Him will praise the LORD.
Let your heart live forever!
All the ends of the world
Shall remember and turn to the LORD,
And all the families of the nations
Shall worship before You.
For the kingdom is the LORD's,
And He rules over the nations.
[verses 16–24, 26–28]

*I have called on You repeatedly, Lord,
to deliver me from people and circumstances
and You have responded. But I never have
responded adequately to You.
I have failed to acknowledge your goodness
publicly, missing the opportunity
to encourage others with the news
of Your workings.
Things will be different from now on.* —SB

My Shepherd

The LORD is my shepherd; I shall not want.
He makes me to lie down in green pastures;
He leads me beside the still waters.
He restores my soul;
He leads me in the paths of righteousness
For His name's sake.
Yea, though I walk through the valley
of the shadow of death,
I will fear no evil;
For You are with me;
Your rod and Your staff, they comfort me.
You prepare a table before me in the
presence of my enemies;
You anoint my head with oil;
My cup runs over.
Surely goodness and mercy shall follow me
All the days of my life;
And I will dwell in the house of the LORD
Forever.

*Sheep are lost without a shepherd, but even
"found" sheep need to be taught how to follow.
In Eastern countries, a shepherd—
concerned for the safety of the lamb that
consistently wanders away— uses
his rod of correction
to break the animal's leg. Then the shepherd
carries the hurt one close to his heart
until the bone mends. There is no more
wandering after that! —JB*

The Earth Is the LORD'S

The earth is the LORD'S, and all its fullness,
The world and those who dwell therein.
For He has founded it upon the seas,
And established it upon the waters.
Who may ascend into the hill of the LORD?
Or who may stand in His holy place?
He who has clean hands and a pure heart,
Who has not lifted up his soul to an idol,
Nor sworn deceitfully.
He shall receive blessing from the LORD,
And righteousness from the God of his salvation.
This is Jacob, the generation of those who seek Him,
Who seek Your face.   Selah
Lift up your heads, O you gates!
And be lifted up, you everlasting doors!
And the King of glory shall come in.
Who is this King of glory?
The LORD strong and mighty,
The LORD mighty in battle.
Lift up your heads, O you gates!
And lift them up, you everlasting doors!
And the King of glory shall come in.
Who is this King of glory?
The LORD of hosts,
He is the King of glory.   Selah

He designed it, and He will finish it. This world!
Whatever He starts, He finishes, for He is not
like us. Have you ever seen a half made moon,
an unfinished star, or a sketchy sunset?
He will just as surely finish His work
on those of us who dwell in His holy temple.
People like you, and people like me! —JB

He restores my soul;
He leads me in the paths
of righteousness
For His name's sake.

Teach Me Your Paths

To You, O Lord, I lift up my soul.
O my God, I trust in You;
Let me not be ashamed;
Let not my enemies triumph over me.
Indeed, let no one who waits on You
be ashamed;
Let those be ashamed who deal
treacherously without cause.
Show me Your ways, O Lord;
Teach me Your paths.
Lead me in Your truth and teach me,
For You are the God of my salvation;
On You I wait all the day.
Remember, O Lord, Your tender
mercies and Your lovingkindnesses,
For they have been from of old.
Do not remember the sins of my
youth, nor my transgressions;
According to Your mercy remember me,
For Your goodness' sake, O Lord.

Looking back over my life,
I see many things for which I am ashamed.
I freely confess my sins
and seek Your forgiveness.
Looking ahead, I sense
the dreaded possibilities
of danger and defeat.
Promise to me, Lord, for the future,
the same love and goodness with which
You have forgiven my past. —SB

From PSALM 25

I Put My Trust in You

Good and upright is the LORD;
Therefore He teaches sinners in the way.
The humble He guides in justice,
And the humble He teaches His way.
All the paths of the Lord are mercy and truth,
To such as keep His covenant and His testimonies.
For Your name's sake, O LORD,
Pardon my iniquity, for it is great.
Who is the man that fears the LORD?
Him shall He teach in the way He chooses.
He himself shall dwell in prosperity,
And his descendants shall inherit the earth.
The secret of the LORD is with those who fear Him,
And He will show them His covenant.
My eyes are ever toward the LORD,
For He shall pluck my feet out of the net.
Turn Yourself to me, and have mercy on me,
For I am desolate and afflicted.
The troubles of my heart have enlarged;
Oh, bring me out of my distresses!
Look on my affliction and my pain,
And forgive all my sins.
Consider my enemies, for they are many;
And they hate me with cruel hatred.
Oh, keep my soul, and deliver me;
Let me not be ashamed,
for I put my trust in You.
Let integrity and uprightness preserve me,
For I wait for You.
Redeem Israel, O God,
Out of all their troubles!

The path of life which I travel daily
is no place for an arrogant man.
Hills too steep, ditches too deep,
corners too sharp, stretches too dark
fill the journey with danger and difficulty.
Your guidance alone makes the journey safe,
but it takes a humble man to admit this,
and an obedient man to claim the benefits.
Help me to be that man. —SB

Temple Keepers

Vindicate me, O LORD,
for I have walked in my integrity.
I have also trusted in the LORD; I shall not slip.
Examine me, O LORD, and prove me;
try my mind and my heart.
For Your lovingkindness is before my eyes,
and I have walked in Your truth.
I have not sat with idolatrous mortals,
nor will I go in with hypocrites.
I have hated the congregation of evildoers,
and will not sit with the wicked.
I will wash my hands in innocence;
so I will go about Your altar, O LORD,
that I may proclaim with the voice of thanksgiving,
and tell of all Your wondrous works.
LORD, I have loved the habitation of Your house,
and the place where Your glory dwells.
Do not gather my soul together with sinners,
nor my life with bloodthirsty men,
in whose hands is a sinister scheme,
and whose right hand is full of bribes.
But as for me, I will walk in my integrity;
redeem me and be merciful to me.
My foot stands in an even place;
in the congregations I will bless the LORD.

*The psalmist David said that he loved
the habitation of the Lord,
where His glory dwelt. The apostle Paul
wrote that the Christian's body is
the habitation of the Holy Spirit,
and His glory dwells there.
Are we good temple keepers?
Do we tell others about
our indwelling Lord?* —JB

From PSALM 27

Wait on the LORD

The LORD is my light and my salvation;
Whom shall I fear?
The LORD is the strength of my life;
Of whom shall I be afraid?
When the wicked came against me
To eat up my flesh,
My enemies and foes,
They stumbled and fell.
Though an army should encamp against me,
My heart shall not fear;
Though war should rise against me,
In this I will be confident.
One thing I have desired of the LORD,
That will I seek:
That I may dwell in the house of the LORD
All the days of my life,
To behold the beauty of the LORD,
And to inquire in His temple.
For in the time of trouble
He shall hide me in His pavilion;
In the secret place of His tabernacle
He shall hide me;
He shall set me high upon a rock.
And now my head shall be lifted up
above my enemies around me;
Therefore I will offer sacrifices of joy
in His tabernacle;
I will sing, yes, I will sing praises to the LORD. . . .
Wait on the LORD;
Be of good courage,
And He shall strengthen your heart;
Wait, I say, on the LORD! [verses 1–6, 14]

*Fear is a terrible thing. It can paralyze
our faith, reduce us to misery, and spoil
our relationships. We can be afraid
of anybody or anything. We can even fear fear!
The answer lies in a faith which comes by
hearing, and a hearing which comes by
the Word of God. For that faith
we must wait on the Lord.* —JB

Do Not Be Silent

To You I will cry, O LORD my Rock:
Do not be silent to me,
Lest, if You are silent to me,
I become like those who go down to the pit.
Hear the voice of my supplications
When I cry to You,
When I lift up my hands toward Your holy sanctuary.
Do not take me away with the wicked
And with the workers of iniquity,
Who speak peace to their neighbors,
But evil is in their hearts.
Give to them according to their deeds,
And according to the wickedness of
their endeavors;
Give to them according to the work of their hands;
Render to them what they deserve.
Because they do not regard the works of the LORD,
Nor the operation of His hands,
He shall destroy them
And not build them up.
Blessed be the LORD,
Because He has heard the voice of my
supplications!
The LORD is my strength and my shield;
My heart trusted in Him, and I am helped;
Therefore my heart greatly rejoices,
And with my song I will praise Him.
The LORD is their strength,
And He is the saving refuge of His anointed.
Save Your people,
And bless Your inheritance;
Shepherd them also,
And bear them up forever.

I fear for those who ignore and deny You,
Lord. They will suffer the consequences
of their self-sufficiency and bear the brunt
of Your offended righteousness.
In my weakness I am anything but
self-sufficient. I acknowledge my frailty,
I crave Your support, I long for
Your protection, I plead for Your help. —SB

The Voice of the LORD

Give unto the LORD, O you mighty ones,
Give unto the LORD glory and strength.
Give unto the LORD the glory due to His name;
Worship the LORD in the beauty of holiness.
The voice of the LORD is over the waters;
The God of glory thunders;
The LORD is over many waters.
The voice of the LORD is powerful;
The voice of the LORD is full of majesty.
The voice of the LORD breaks the cedars,
Yes, the LORD splinters the cedars of Lebanon.
He makes them also skip like a calf,
Lebanon and Sirion like a young wild ox.
The voice of the LORD divides the flames of fire.
The voice of the LORD shakes the wilderness;
The LORD shakes the Wilderness of Kadesh.
The voice of the LORD makes the deer give birth,
And strips the forests bare;
And in His temple everyone says, "Glory!"
The LORD sat enthroned at the Flood,
And the LORD sits as King forever.
The LORD will give strength to His people;
The LORD will bless His people with peace.

I need to be reminded of Your greatness, Lord,
and reminders abound. On the beach I hear
the rolling breakers, in the forest I see
mighty trees split by lightning,
in the cool glades I see a timid doe
with fragile offspring. On every hand
I rejoice in the boundless evidence
of Your great presence. You speak to me. —SB

Joy Comes in the Morning

I will extol You, O LORD,
for You have lifted me up,
And have not let my foes rejoice over me.
O LORD my God, I cried out to You,
And You have healed me.
O LORD, You have brought my soul up
from the grave;
You have kept me alive, that I should
not go down to the pit.
Sing praise to the LORD, You saints of His,
And give thanks at the remembrance of
His holy name.
For His anger is but for a moment,
His favor is for life;
Weeping may endure for a night,
But joy comes in the morning.
Now in my prosperity I said,
"I shall never be moved."
LORD, by Your favor You have made
my mountain stand strong;
You hid Your face, and I was troubled.
I cried out to You, O LORD;
And to the LORD I made supplication:
"What profit is there in my blood,
When I go down to the pit?
Will the dust praise You?
Will it declare Your truth?
Hear, O LORD, and have mercy on me;
LORD, be my helper!"
You have turned for me my mourning
into dancing;
You have put off my sackcloth and
clothed me with gladness,
To the end that my glory may sing
praise to You and not be silent.
O LORD my God, I will give thanks to
You forever.

Some say that Christians shouldn't cry.
We have to ask then how it was that
"Jesus wept"?
The Potter cannot mold the clay
unless it is moist. If we are bathed
in tears, the Father can reshape the raw edges
and smooth out our life again.
It will be finished by morning.
Joy shall awaken us to praise! —JB

I will bless the LORD
at all times;
His praise shall continually
be in my mouth.

From PSALM 31

My Rock and Fortress

In You, O Lord, I put my trust;
Let me never be ashamed;
Deliver me in Your righteousness.
Bow down Your ear to me,
Deliver me speedily;
Be my rock of refuge,
A fortress of defense to save me.
For You are my rock and my fortress;
Therefore, for Your name's sake,
Lead me and guide me.
Pull me out of the net which they have
secretly laid for me,
For You are my strength.
Into Your hand I commit my spirit;
You have redeemed me, O Lord God of truth.
I have hated those who regard vain idols;
But I trust in the Lord.
I will be glad and rejoice in Your mercy,
For You have considered my trouble;
You have known my soul in adversities,
And have not shut me up into the
hand of the enemy;
You have set my feet in a wide place.
Have mercy on me, O Lord,
for I am in trouble;
My eye wastes away with grief,
Yes, my soul and my body!
For my life is spent with grief,
And my years with sighing;
My strength fails because of my iniquity,
And my bones waste away. [verses 1–10]

*When we cannot praise Him for what He has
allowed, let us praise Him for "Who He is"
in what He has allowed. He has promised
to give us "beauty for ashes, the oil of joy
for mourning, and the garment of praise
for our spirit of heaviness."* —JB

From PSALM 31

In Your Hand

But as for me, I trust in You, O Lord;
I say, "You are my God."
My times are in Your hand;
Deliver me from the hand of my enemies.
And from those who persecute me.
Make Your face shine upon Your servant;
Save me for Your mercies' sake.
Do not let me be ashamed, O Lord,
for I have called upon You;
Let the wicked be ashamed;
Let them be silent in the grave.
Let the lying lips be put to silence,
Which speak insolent things proudly and
contemptuously against the righteous.
Oh, how great is Your goodness,
Which You have laid up for those who fear You,
Which You have prepared for those who trust in You
In the presence of the sons of men!
You shall hide them in the secret place
of Your presence
From the plots of man;
You shall keep them secretly in a pavilion
From the strife of tongues.
Blessed be the Lord,
For He has shown me His marvelous
kindness in a strong city!
For I said in my haste,
"I am cut off from before Your eyes";
Nevertheless You heard the voice of
my supplications
When I cried out to You.
Oh, love the Lord, all you His saints!
For the Lord preserves the faithful,
And fully repays the proud person.
Be of good courage,
And He shall strengthen your heart,
All you who hope in the Lord. [verses 14–24]

I've two choices—either to hold my life
in my hands or to place it in Yours.
The choice seems easy, for how can
the strength in my arms compare to the might
of Your fingers? Yet, in my stubbornness
I still struggle to ensure that I am
committed continually to You. —SB

From PSALM 32

My Hiding Place

Blessed is he whose transgression is forgiven,
Whose sin is covered.
Blessed is the man to whom the LORD
does not impute iniquity,
And in whose spirit there is no guile.
When I kept silent, my bones grew old
Through my groaning all the day long.
For day and night Your hand was heavy upon me;
My vitality was turned into the
drought of summer.   Selah
I acknowledged my sin to You,
And my iniquity I have not hidden.
I said, "I will confess my transgressions
to the LORD,"
And You forgave the iniquity of my sin.   Selah
For this cause everyone who is godly
shall pray to You
In a time when You may be found;
Surely in a flood of great waters
They shall not come near him.
You are my hiding place;
You shall preserve me from trouble;
You shall surround me with songs of
deliverance.   Selah
I will instruct you and teach you in the
way you should go;
I will guide you with My eye. [verses 1–8]

Confession was good for my soul.
When I tried to excuse my sin
or hide the truth of my actions,
I was like a dried-up riverbed.
But Your Spirit led me to repentance, and
the floods of Your forgiveness flowed.
Now, having learned that much, I eagerly
look forward to new things
You will pour into my life. —SB

From PSALM 33

Sing a New Song

Rejoice in the LORD, O you righteous!
For praise from the upright is beautiful.
Praise the LORD with the harp;
Make melody to Him with an
instrument of ten strings.
Sing to Him a new song;
Play skillfully with a shout of joy.
For the word of the LORD is right,
And all His work is done in truth.
He loves righteousness and justice;
The earth is full of the goodness of the LORD.
By the word of the LORD the heavens were made,
And all the host of them by the breath of His mouth.
He gathers the waters of the sea together as a heap;
He lays up the deep in storehouses.
Let all the earth fear the LORD;
Let all the inhabitants of the world
stand in awe of Him.
For he spoke, and it was done;
He commanded, and it stood fast.
The LORD brings the counsel of the
nations to nothing;
He makes the plans of the peoples of no effect.
The counsel of the LORD stands forever,
The plans of His heart to all generations.
Blessed is the nation whose God is the LORD,
And the people whom He has chosen as
His own inheritance.

*If we are in tune with the Lord, we will
not be "sung out." We will sing a new song!
There certainly will be a symphony in our
souls if we allow the Maker of Music to
"conduct" our lives. He will fill our days
with the happiest of melodies. Sing out,
others may catch the rhythm. Maybe we can
even teach our world to sing again!* —JB

From PSALM 33

He Is Our Help and Shield

The Lord looks from heaven;
He sees all the sons of men.
From the place of His habitation He looks
On all the inhabitants of the earth;
He fashions their hearts individually;
He considers all their works.
There is no king saved by the multitude of an army;
A mighty man is not delivered by great strength.
A horse is a vain hope for safety;
Neither shall it deliver any by its great strength.
Behold, the eye of the Lord is on
those who fear Him,
On those who hope in His mercy,
To deliver their soul from death,
And to keep them alive in famine.
Our soul waits for the Lord;
He is our help and our shield.
For our heart shall rejoice in Him,
Because we have trusted in His holy name.
Let Your mercy, O Lord, be upon us,
Just as we hope in You.

We humans are body, soul, and spirit.
God is able to "deliver our soul from death."
He does this by asking us to receive
His risen Son, the Lord Jesus Christ,
into our hearts. If we receive Him
"our hearts shall rejoice," for eternal life
is the very life of the Eternal One! —JB

From PSALM 34

I Love to Praise You

I will bless the LORD at all times;
His praise shall continually be in my mouth.
My soul shall make its boast in the LORD;
The humble shall hear of it and be glad.
Oh, magnify the LORD with me,
And let us exalt His name together.
I sought the LORD, and He heard me,
And delivered me from all my fears.
They looked to Him and were radiant,
And their faces were not ashamed.
This poor man cried out,
and the LORD heard him,
And saved him out of all his troubles.
The angel of the LORD encamps
around those who fear Him,
And delivers them.
Oh, taste and see that the LORD is good;
Blessed is the man who trusts in Him!
Oh, fear the LORD, you His saints!
There is no want to those who fear Him.
The young lions lack and suffer hunger;
But those who seek the LORD shall not
lack any good thing.

I love to praise You, Lord, because it is
a natural expression of my experience of You.
Your goodness amazes and thrills me. I have
learned that my praises delight You,
and that makes me want to delight
You even more.
I have learned that my praises can light
a fire in other people—a fire that leads
them to know You and praise You.
Praise You that I can praise! —SB

From PSALM 34

Come, Children

Come, you children, listen to me;
I will teach you the fear of the LORD.
Who is the man who desires life,
And loves many days, that he may see good?
Keep your tongue from evil,
And your lips from speaking guile.
Depart from evil, and do good;
Seek peace, and pursue it.
The eyes of the LORD are on the righteous,
And His ears are open to their cry.
The face of the LORD is against those who do evil,
To cut off the remembrance of them from the earth.
The righteous cry out, and the LORD hears,
And delivers them out of all their troubles.
The LORD is near to those who have a broken heart,
And saves such as have a contrite spirit.
Many are the afflictions of the righteous,
But the LORD delivers him out of them all.
He guards all his bones;
Not one of them is broken.
Evil shall slay the wicked,
And those who hate the righteous shall
be condemned.
The LORD redeems the soul of His servants,
And none of those who trust in Him
shall be condemned.

How teachable are the little ones.
Their natural curiosity, their sense of wonder
at the unfolding mysteries of their world can
lead to tender hearts and open minds.
Lord, help me teach them Your truth,
so they may learn early of Your grace
and forgiveness. —SB

*For His anger
is but for a moment,
His favor is for life.*

om PSALM 35

‑ORD, Who Is Like You?

‑ead my cause, O LORD, with those
‑no strive with me;
‑ght against those who fight against me.
‑ke hold of shield and buckler,
‑nd stand up for my help.
‑lso draw out the spear,
‑nd stop those who pursue me.
‑ay to my soul,
‑ am your salvation."
‑et those be put to shame and brought to dishonor
‑ho seek after my life;
‑et those be turned back and brought to confusion
‑ho plot my hurt.
‑et them be like chaff before the wind,
‑nd let the angel of the LORD chase them.
‑et their way be dark and slippery,
‑nd let the angel of the LORD pursue them.
‑or without cause they have hidden
‑eir net for me in a pit,
‑Which they have dug without cause for my life.
‑et destruction come upon him unexpectedly,
‑nd let his net that he has hidden catch himself;
‑nto that very destruction let him fall.
‑nd my soul shall be joyful in the LORD;
‑ shall rejoice in His salvation.
‑ll my bones shall say,
‑ORD, who is like You,
‑elivering the poor from him who is
‑o strong for him,
‑es, the poor and the needy from him
‑ho plunders him?"

‑ometimes our circumstances reduce us
‑o complete dependence upon the Lord.
‑hen we find out there is no one quite like Him.
‑Ve can hang our weakness upon His strength,
‑ur inability upon His power, our helplessness
‑pon His help and prove Him mighty
‑ndeed to save. —JB

From PSALM 35

You Are My Rescue

Fierce witnesses rise up;
They ask me things that I do not know.
They reward me evil for good,
To the sorrow of my soul.
But as for me, when they were sick,
My clothing was sackcloth;
I humbled myself with fasting;
And my prayer would return to my own heart.
I paced about as though he were my
friend or brother;
I bowed down heavily, as one who
mourns for his mother.
But in my adversity they rejoiced
And gathered together;
Attackers gathered against me,
And I did not know it;
They tore at me and did not cease;
With ungodly mockers at feasts
They gnashed at me with their teeth.
LORD, how long will You look on?
Rescue me from the destructions,
My precious life from the lions.
I will give You thanks in the great congregation;
I will praise You among many people.

Some people are giving me a hard time, Lor
Rescue me from returning evil for evil.
Help me to overcome wrong with right,
and remind me that I am responsible only
for my actions. —JB

From PSALM 35

The Sparkle of Your Glory

Let them not rejoice over me who are
wrongfully my enemies;
Nor let them wink with the eye who
hate me without a cause.
For they do not speak peace,
But they devise deceitful matters
Against those who are quiet in the land.
They also opened their mouth wide against me,
And said, "Aha, aha!
Our eyes have seen it."
This You have seen, O Lord;
Do not keep silence.
O Lord, do not be far from me.
Stir up Yourself, and awake to my vindication,
To my cause, my God and my Lord.
Vindicate me, O Lord my God,
According to Your righteousness;
And let them not rejoice over me.
Let them not say in their hearts,
"Ah, so we would have it!"
Let them not say,
"We have swallowed him up."
Let them be ashamed and brought to
mutual confusion
Who rejoice at my hurt;
Let them be clothed with shame and dishonor
Who magnify themselves against me.
Let them shout for joy and be glad,
Who favor my righteous cause;
And let them say continually,
"Let the Lord be magnified,
Who has pleasure in the prosperity of
His servant."
And my tongue shall speak of Your
righteousness
And of Your praise all the day long.

Sometimes I feel
as if my world is a swamp—
sullen, stagnant, and stale. But then I see
the sun touch the water with the sparkle
of Your glory, and the slender reeds of
changed lives grow straight and succulent.
I marvel again at Your greatness. —SB

The Fountain of Life

An oracle within my heart concerning
the transgression of the wicked:
There is no fear of God before his eyes.
For he flatters himself in his own eyes,
When he finds out his iniquity and when he hates.
The words of his mouth are wickedness and deceit;
He has ceased to be wise and to do good.
He devises wickedness on his bed;
He sets himself in a way that is not good;
He does not abhor evil.
Your mercy, O Lord, is in the heavens,
And Your faithfulness reaches to the clouds.
Your righteousness is like the great mountains;
Your judgments are a great deep;
O Lord, You preserve man and beast.
How precious is Your lovingkindness, O God!
Therefore the children of men put their trust
under the shadow of Your wings.
They are abundantly satisfied with the
fullness of Your house,
And You give them drink from the
river of Your pleasures.
For with You is the fountain of life;
In Your light we see light.
Oh, continue Your lovingkindness to
those who know You,
And Your righteousness to the upright in heart.
[verses 1–10]

The fountain of life springs from You,
dear Lord, giving hope to us
for fullness of life and depth of truth.
In our world meaning has been polluted.
The human stream is littered with
the tangled garbage of a million broken lives.
The waters of life reek with the stench of iniquity.
How we need the cleansing flow of
Your Holy Spirit,
the wholesome flood of Your truth. —SB

From PSALM 37

Rest in the LORD

Do not fret because of evildoers,
Nor be envious of the workers of iniquity.
For they shall soon be cut down like the grass,
And wither as the green herb.
Trust in the LORD, and do good;
Dwell in the land, and feed on His
faithfulness.
Delight yourself also in the LORD,
And He shall give you the desires of your heart.
Commit your way to the LORD,
Trust also in Him,
And He shall bring it to pass.
He shall bring forth your
righteousness as the light,
And your justice as the noonday.
Rest in the LORD, and wait patiently for Him;
Do not fret because of him who
prospers in his way,
Because of the man who brings wicked
schemes to pass.
Cease from anger, and forsake wrath;
Do not fret—it only causes harm.
For evildoers shall be cut off;
But those who wait on the LORD,
They shall inherit the earth.
For yet a little while and the wicked
shall be no more;
Indeed, you will look diligently for his place,
But it shall be no more.
But the meek shall inherit the earth,
And shall delight themselves
in the abundance of peace. [verses 1–11]

Resting in the Lord
does not mean inactivity or leisure.
Resting means quiet power in action.
The Holy Spirit enables us to stop worrying
and turn our terror into thoughtful deeds.
Patience is love waiting out suffering;
resting is trusting in
the sovereignty of God. —JB

From PSALM 37

He Is Ever Merciful

A little that a righteous man has
Is better than the riches of many wicked.
For the arms of the wicked shall be broken,
But the LORD upholds the righteous.
The LORD knows the days of the upright,
And their inheritance shall be forever.
They shall not be ashamed in the evil time,
And in the days of famine they shall be satisfied.
But the wicked shall perish;
And the enemies of the LORD,
Like the splendor of the meadows, shall vanish.
Into smoke they shall vanish away.
The wicked borrows and does not repay,
But the righteous shows mercy and gives.
For those who are blessed by Him
shall inherit the earth,
But those who are cursed by Him shall be cut off.
The steps of a good man are ordered
by the LORD,
And he delights in his way.
Though he fall,
he shall not be utterly cast down;
For the LORD upholds him with His hand.
I have been young, and now am old;
Yet I have not seen the righteous forsaken,
Nor his descendants begging bread.
He is ever merciful, and lends;
And his descendants are blessed. [verses 16–26]

God blesses us with things. *We must make sure we possess our possessions, not that they possess us! It is God who gives us power to get wealth. Lord, make us good stewards.* —JB

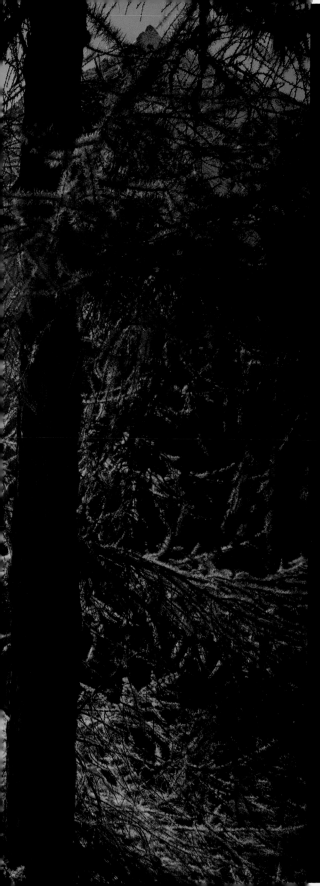

From PSALM 37

The Righteous Inherit the Land

Depart from evil, and do good;
And dwell forevermore.
For the LORD loves justice,
And does not forsake His saints;
They are preserved forever,
But the descendants of the wicked shall be cut off.
The righteous shall inherit the land,
And dwell in it forever.
The mouth of the righteous speaks wisdom,
And his tongue talks of justice.
The law of his God is in his heart;
None of his steps shall slide.
The wicked watches the righteous,
And seeks to slay him.
The LORD will not leave him in his hand,
Nor condemn him when he is judged.
Wait on the LORD, and keep His way,
And He shall exalt you to inherit the land;
When the wicked are cut off, you shall see it.
I have seen the wicked in great power,
And spreading himself like a native green tree.
Yet he passed away, and behold, he was no more;
Indeed I sought him, but he could not be found.
Mark the blameless man, and observe the upright;
For the future of that man is peace.
But the transgressors shall be destroyed together;
The future of the wicked shall be cut off.
But the salvation of the righteous is
from the LORD;
He is their strength in the time of trouble.
[verses 27–39]

Wicked men have terrorized the world
in my lifetime, Lord. At the zenith of
their power, they were awesome; but now
they are gone. Like great trees they
towered over their contemporaries; now like
rotting logs they lie forgotten.
Lord, You brought them low. I'm glad I didn't
fear or follow them but waited for You to act.—SB

The earth is the LORD's,
and all its fullness,
The world and those
who dwell therein.

From PSALM 38

Stand Tall Beside Me

O LORD, do not rebuke me in Your wrath,
Nor chasten me in Your hot displeasure!
For Your arrows pierce me deeply,
And Your hand presses me down.
There is no soundness in my flesh
Because of Your anger,
Nor is there any health in my bones
Because of my sin.
For my iniquities have gone over my head;
Like a heavy burden they are too heavy for me.
My wounds are foul and festering
Because of my foolishness.
I am troubled, I am bowed down greatly;
I go mourning all the day long.
For my loins are full of inflammation,
And there is no soundness in my flesh.
I am feeble and severely broken;
I groan because of the turmoil of my heart.
Lord, all my desire is before You;
And my sighing is not hidden from You.
My heart pants, my strength fails me;
As for the light of my eyes,
it also has gone from me.
My loved ones and my friends stand
aloof from my plague,
And my kinsmen stand afar off.

In my pain and loneliness,
life has become bleak and cold.
I sense Your displeasure.
I know my faults, and I turn to You.
Bring strength to my weakness,
warmth to the coldness.
Though my friends may fail,
please stand tall and straight
beside me, Lord. —SB

From PSALM 38

In You I Hope

Those also who seek my life lay snares for me;
Those who seek my hurt speak of destruction,
And plan deception all the day long.
But I, like a deaf man, do not hear;
And I am like a mute who does not open his mouth.
Thus I am like a man who does not hear,
And in whose mouth is no response.
For in You, O LORD, I hope;
You will hear, O Lord my God.
For I said, "Hear me,
lest they rejoice over me,
Lest, when my foot slips,
they magnify themselves against me."
For I am ready to fall,
And my sorrow is continually before me.
For I will declare my iniquity;
I will be in anguish over my sin.
But my enemies are vigorous,
and they are strong;
And those who hate me wrongfully
have multiplied.
Those also who render evil for good,
They are my adversaries, because I
follow what is good.
Do not forsake me, O LORD;
O my God, be not far from me!
Make haste to help me,
O Lord, my salvation!

If God be for us, who can be against us?
He knows our heart, so why not leave
the conclusion of circumstances with Him?
Our job is to live rightly and not respond
wrongly to those who don't —JB

Hear My Prayer

I said, "I will guard my ways,
Lest I sin with my tongue;
I will restrain my mouth with a muzzle,
While the wicked are before me."
I was mute with silence,
I held my peace even from good;
And my sorrow was stirred up.
My heart was hot within me;
While I was musing the fire burned.
Then I spoke with my tongue:
"LORD, make me to know my end,
And what is the measure of my days,
That I may know how frail I am.
Indeed, You have made my days as
handbreadths,
And my age is as nothing before You;
Certainly every man at his best state is
but vapor.   Selah
Surely every man walks about like a shadow;
Surely they busy themselves in vain;
He heaps up riches,
And does not know who will gather them.
"And now, LORD, what do I wait for?
My hope is in You.
Deliver me from all my transgressions;
Do not make me the reproach of the
foolish. . . .
Hear my prayer, O LORD,
And give ear to my cry;
Do not be silent at my tears;
For I am a stranger with You,
A sojourner, as all my fathers were.
Remove Your gaze from me,
that I may regain strength,
Before I go away and am no more."
[verses 1–8, 12–13]

Like grass in the desert burned and barren,
I struggle sometimes to survive.
In the past I tried to do it alone.
I resisted my pain, I resented
what I perceived You had done. The heat
intensified, the desert sand covered me.
But I turned to You, Lord.
You alone were my hope. —SB

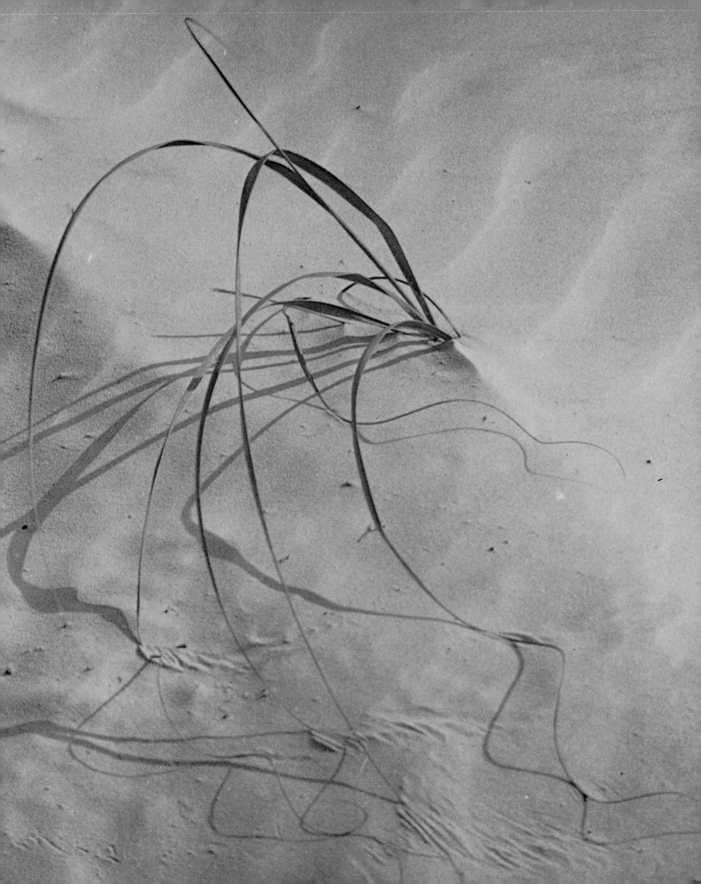

By the word of the Lord
the heavens were made.

Photos by: Page:

Stockphotos International: 1.
Robert Cushman Hayes: 6–7, 11, 12–13, 14, 15, 24–25, 26, 27,
                        43, 44, 45, 62, 63, 50, 64, 74, 75.
Walter Studer: 8–9, 10, 70, 71.
Zefa: 16–17.
Willi P. Burkhardt: 18–19, 20–21, 28–29, 34–35, 40–41, 52–53,
                     66–67, 68–69, 76–77.
Flemming Walsøe: 22, 60–61.
Benny Alex: 23, 51, 56.
Otto Pfenniger: 30–31, 72–73.
Jørgen Vium Olesen: 32–33, 42, 54, 55, 57, 58, 59.
Siegfried Eigstler: 36–37, 38–39, 46–47.
Colour Library International: 48–49.